Animal Homes

Deserts

By John Wood

BookLife

©2018
Book Life
King's Lynn
Norfolk PE30 4LS

ISBN: 978-1-78637-134-8

All rights reserved
Printed in Malaysia

Written by:
John Wood

Edited by:
Holly Duhig

Designed by:
Matt Rumbelow

A catalogue record for this book is available from the British Library.

Photocredits: Abbreviations: l-left, r-right, b-bottom, t-top, c-centre, m-middle. Images are courtesy of Shutterstock.com. With thanks to Getty Images, Thinkstock Photo and iStockphoto. Covertr – iFtLizard, Covertm – Francois van Heerden, Covertl – Jacopo Werther, Coverbl – kamon_saejueng, Coverbr – Wolfgang Zwanzger 2 – Perfect Lazybones. 3: bg – nontthepcool; front – Banana Republic images. 4 – Debbie Steinhausser. 5: bg – smikeymikey1; tl – bikeriderlondon; tr – Ehrman Photographic; m – Banana Republic images; bl – Joe Belanger; br – GUDKOV ANDREY. 6 – Perfect Lazybones. 7 – Jamie Ahmad. 8: bg – Elena Badamshina; tl – Rosalie Kreulen; tr – Villiers Steyn; br - Don Mammoser; 9 – Fotografie-Kuhlmann. 10 – Kris Wiktor. 11 – bierchen. 12 – Peter Barrett. 13 – Alta Oosthuizen. 14 – pixy. 15 – Jason Mintzer. 16 – Matt Jeppson. 17 – Matt Jeppson. 18 – Dmitry Rukhlenko. 19 – Vixit. 20 – LanaElcova. 21 – Ammak. 22 – SeraphP. 23 - Jez Bennett.

CONTENTS

Page 4	What Is a Habitat?
Page 6	What Is a Desert?
Page 8	Types of Desert Habitat
Page 10	Roadrunners
Page 12	Meerkats
Page 14	Fringe-Toed Lizards
Page 16	Shovelnose Snakes
Page 18	Camels
Page 20	Deserts in Danger
Page 22	Endangered Animals
Page 24	Glossary and Index

Words that look like *this* can be found in the glossary on page 24.

WHAT IS A HABITAT?

A habitat is a place where an animal lives. It provides the animal with food, *shelter* and everything else it needs to survive.

There are lots of different habitats in the world. Each one is home to many different animals.

Forests

Deserts

Oceans

Grasslands

Jungles

WHAT IS A DESERT?

A desert is a type of habitat that is very dry and gets very little rain. Deserts can be hot or cold.

Sahara Desert

The biggest cold desert in the world is Antarctica, which is home to the South Pole. The biggest hot desert in the world is the Sahara in Africa.

Antarctica

TYPES OF DESERT HABITAT?

Sand Dunes

Rocky Plains

Oasis

Hot deserts are home to many different habitats. Rocky plains, sand dunes and oases are all homes for desert animals.

Rocky plains are very flat and dusty. Sand dunes are giant hills of sand. Oases are pools of water in the middle of deserts.

Oases are formed by underground streams that push up through the ground.

ROADRUNNERS

Desert habitats are home to lots of different animals. The roadrunner bird makes its home in the branches of cactus plants that grow in rocky plains.

The roadrunner can run up to 40 kilometres per hour!

Roadrunner eating a lizard.

Rocky plains are home to lots of lizards, snakes and spiders, which roadrunners love to eat. This makes rocky plains the perfect home for roadrunners.

MEERKATS

Meerkats like to live in sandy parts of the desert. This is because meerkats make their homes in tunnels under the sand. These tunnels are called burrows.

Meerkat on the lookout for danger

These burrows give the meerkats a place to sleep and look after their young. They also protect the meerkats from predators, such as eagles.

FRINGE-TOED LIZARDS

Fringe-toed lizards make their homes in sand dunes. Their long toes allow them to move easily through the sand.

Fringe-toed lizards sleep in burrows during the winter months. This is called hibernation. Hibernation protects them from the cold winter weather.

Fringe-toed lizard warming itself in the sunshine

SHOVELNOSE SNAKES

Shovelnose snakes also like to live in sand dunes. Their shovel-shaped snouts help them to quickly burrow into the sand. This is known as sand swimming.

Shovelnose Snake

To avoid the heat in the desert, the shovelnose snake sleeps during the day. It comes out and hunts at night when it is cooler.

Many snakes are nocturnal.

CAMELS

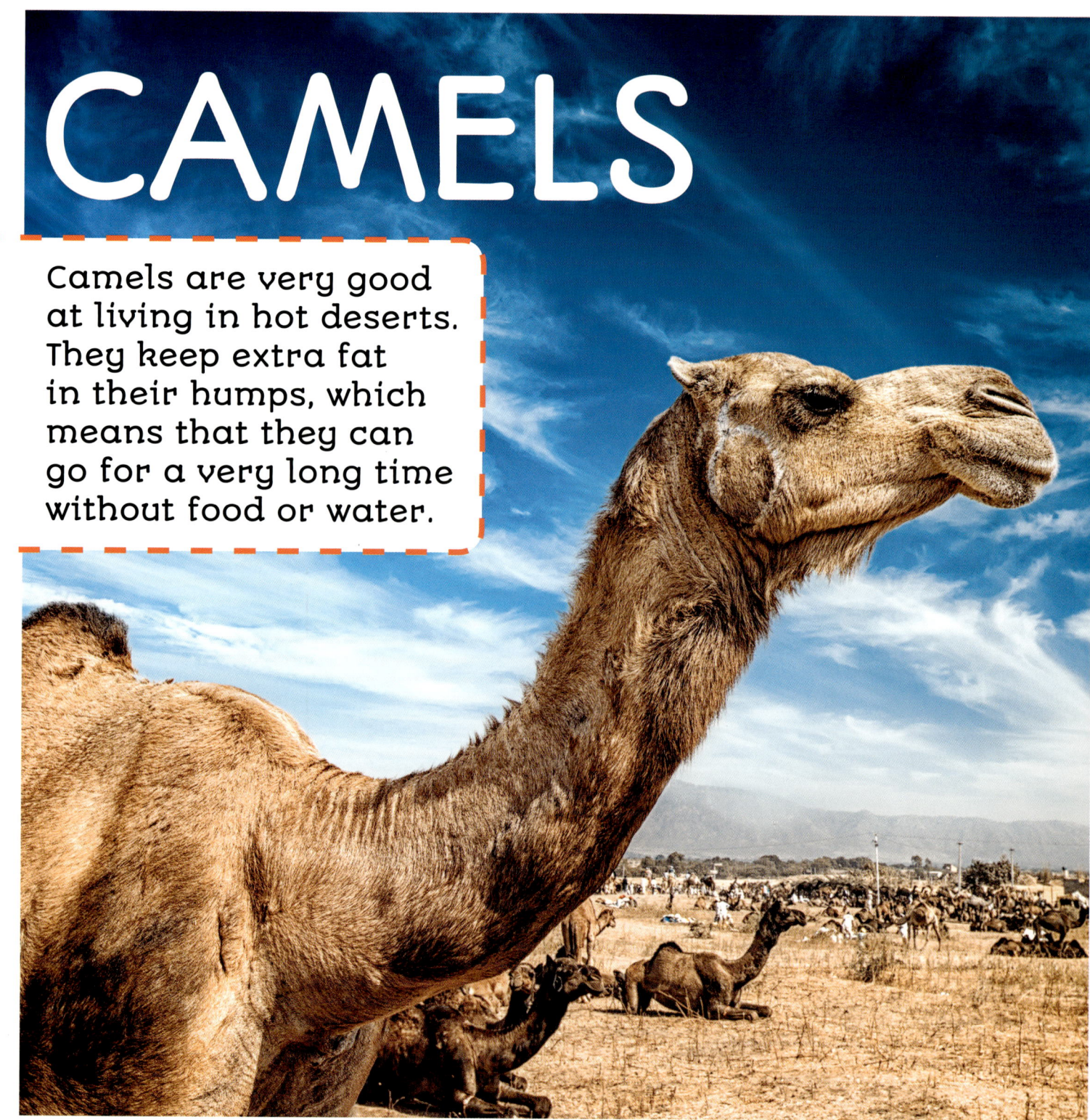

Camels are very good at living in hot deserts. They keep extra fat in their humps, which means that they can go for a very long time without food or water.

People crossing the desert often take camels with them. This is because there is no need to carry extra water for the camels.

People often stop at oases to give their camels a drink.

DESERTS IN DANGER

When harmful *gases* from cars, aeroplanes and factories go into the air, they trap heat on Earth and cause the planet to warm up. This is called global warming and it is putting deserts in danger.

Top Tip! We can help to slow down global warming by walking short journeys instead of using a car.

Global warming can make desert habitats even hotter and drier. This makes it harder for the animals that live in deserts to survive. When an animal is finding it hard to survive, it is said to be endangered.

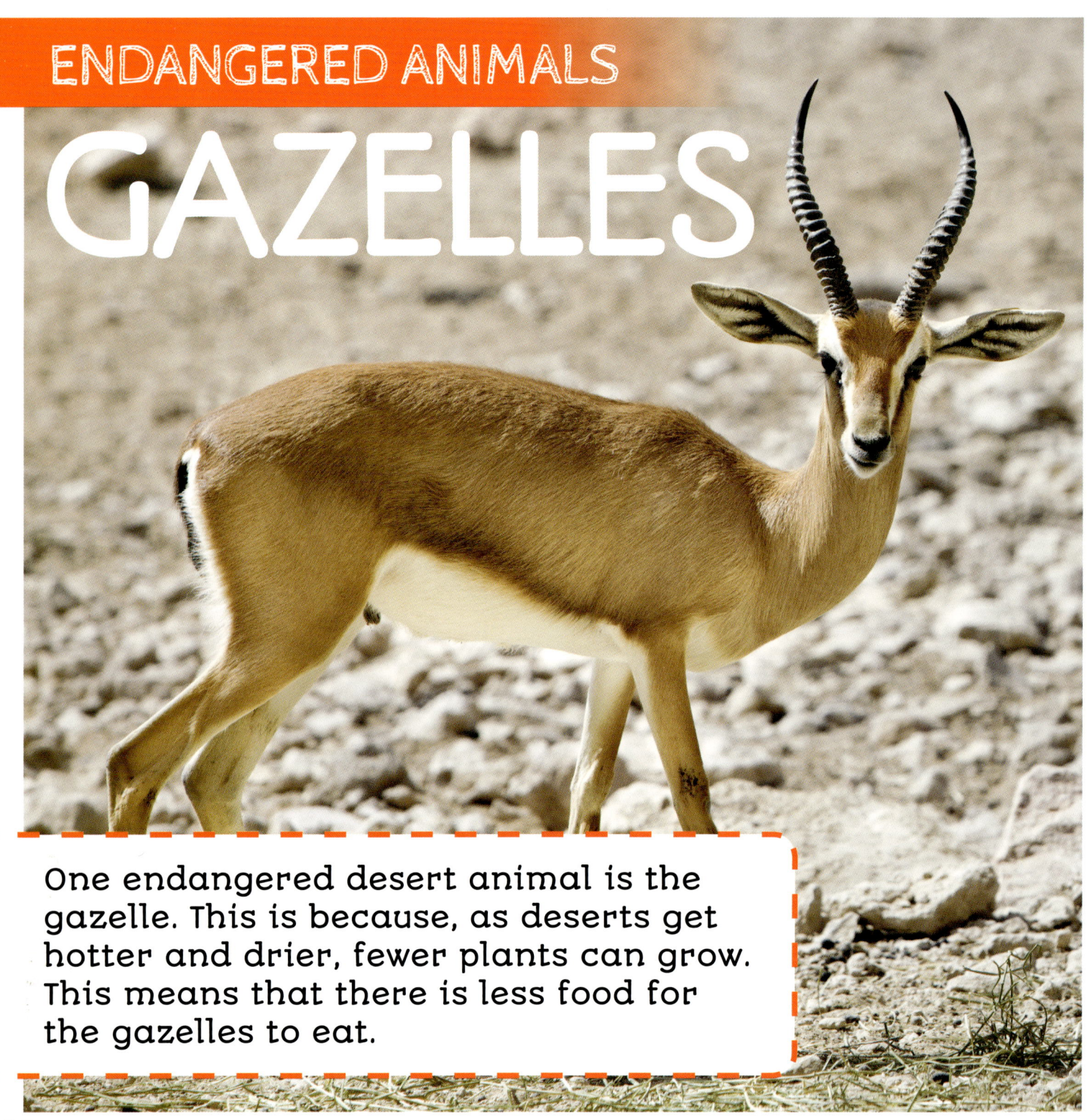

ENDANGERED ANIMALS
GAZELLES

One endangered desert animal is the gazelle. This is because, as deserts get hotter and drier, fewer plants can grow. This means that there is less food for the gazelles to eat.

AFRICAN WILD DOGS

African wild dogs are endangered because people have built lots of houses and roads in their habitat. This means they have less space to hunt for food.

GLOSSARY

endangered	when an animal is in danger of dying out
gases	air-like substances that move around freely
nocturnal	active at night instead of during the day
predators	animals that hunt other animals for food
shelter	protection from danger and harsh weather
snouts	noses and mouths that stick out in front of animals' faces
South Pole	the southernmost point on Earth

Index

Africa 7, 23
burrows 12-13, 15
endangered 21-23
food 4, 18, 22-23
global warming 20-21
oases 8-9, 19

plains 8-11
plants 10, 22
predators 13
sand dunes 8-9, 14, 16
South Pole 7
water 9, 18-19